Our Yard Sale

Practicing the Y Sound

Isabella Garcia

Rosen
PHONICS
READERS

Rosen
Classroom™

My family has a yard sale.

This is our yard.
Come to our yard sale!

We sell yarn.
Do you need yarn?

This yarn is yellow.
Do you like yellow yarn?

We sell yo-yos.
What color are the yo-yos?

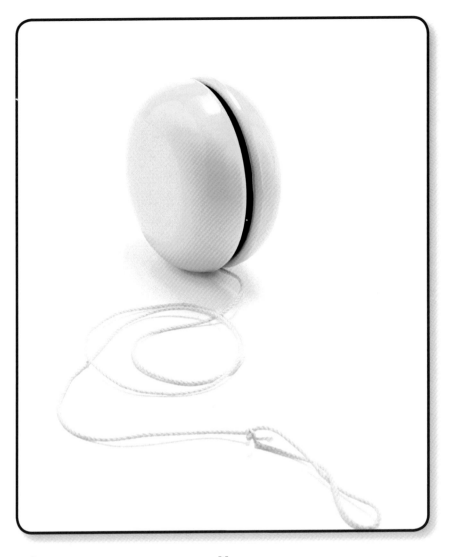

This yo-yo is yellow.
You can use yo-yos to play.

We sell yams.
Yams are yummy!

The yummy yams are
from our garden.

"Yard sale!"
I yell.

Many people stop by our yard.

We have a yard sale
every year!